PET OWNER'S GUIDE TO THE
GOLDFISH

Steve Windsor

RINGPRESS

ABOUT THE AUTHOR

Steve Windsor was educated at Keele University, and the University of Georgia, USA. He has been a magazine journalist for more than 20 years, generally working in areas to do with fish and water.

Steve has written or contributed to six books on fish-related subjects and edited several more, and retains a strong interest in the aquatic world, especially ichthyology and entomology.

Steve is currently Managing Editor of *Practical Fishkeeping,* Britain's best-selling magazine for all-round hobbyist fishkeepers.

ACKNOWLEDGEMENTS

A special thanks to Northern Goldfish and Pondkeepers' Society (Sale, Cheshire), for some of the varieties of goldfish photographed at their 2000 Open Show. Thanks also to the staff of Britain's Aquatic Superstore (Dave's Aquarium) in Bolton, Lancashire, for their kind help and assistance.

PHOTOS

Keith Allison, and courtesy of Tetra UK.

Designed by: Rob Benson

Published by Ringpress Books Limited,
PO Box 8, Lydney, Gloucestershire,
GL15 4YN, United Kingdom.

First published 2002
©2002 Ringpress Books Limited. All rights reserved

ISBN 1 86054 109 7
Printed and bound in Hong Kong through Printworks International Ltd.

CONTENTS

1
Introducing The Goldfish

Goldfish have always been popular. The reason for this long-enduring popularity is easy to understand – goldfish are an adaptable, colourful, and easy-to-care-for addition to any home.

ANCESTORS

The wild cousin of today's pet goldfish is the Crucian carp *(Carassius carassius)*, which is found mainly in the Orient. Except for colour – the Crucian is brown – there is a strong resemblance between the two fish. This has led many people to believe that the Crucian carp is the ancestor of the modern goldfish.

However, there is another contender for the position – the Gibel carp, which shares the goldfish's scientific name *(Carassius auratus)*. This is found eastwards of Poland.

It may be the case that both species have contributed to the gene pool that makes up today's vivid orange-coloured goldfish.

A genetic mutation was responsible for changing the colour of Crucian carp from brown to gold.

Initially, the Japanese concentrated on developing Koi.

EVOLUTION

Goldfish developed in the fish farms of the Far East, where populations of carp were cultivated as a source of food. These captive populations of carp, isolated in the fish farms, evolved into goldfish.

A few individuals underwent a genetic mutation that changed their pigment from brown to gold. When the farmers spotted these differently coloured fish, they isolated them and bred from them – a process called line-breeding.

The coloured fish were mated together, generation after generation, to create a new population of gold-coloured fish. These fish would have been the first members of the common goldfish family.

DEVELOPMENT

The goldfish was 'adopted' by the Japanese in the 16th century. They already had their own fancy carp, the Koi, but, possibly because of their interest in the Koi, it took 200 years before they were breeding and producing their own varieties of goldfish.

Early Japanese breeding concentrated on developing unusual features, such as the hood of the Oranda.

Calico fish were first produced by Japanese breeders.

The 'fancy' goldfish of today are the result of these latter developments in the Japanese fish farms. The Japanese continued the Chinese line-breeding tradition, concentrating on the development of unusual features, such as the hood or wen of the Oranda (see page 17).

The Japanese also bred different colours of goldfish. There is evidence that silver, black, and calico-coloured fish were produced.

Goldfish arrived in the UK in the 18th century. They may not have been the first ornamental fish brought into England as part of the burgeoning trade with the Middle and Far East (the first specially imported fish is thought to have been one of the species of Paradise fish), but they were far more likely to survive in the British climate.

Over the next 300 years, line-breeding in England produced at least one new variety, the Bristol Shubunkin. By the late 1800s, there were goldfish farms in the USA, and the fish had reached Australia.

A programme of line-breeding resulted in the Bristol Shubunkin.

INTRODUCING THE GOLDFISH

Goldfish kept in captivity have a longer life-expectancy than their wild counterparts.

WILD COUSINS

The Crucian and the Gibel are the closest wild relatives of the goldfish, sharing many of its characteristics.

The Crucian and Gibel prefer still water or slow-flowing rivers, and they dislike high levels of oxygen. During the winter months, they slip into semi-hibernation, sinking to the bottom of the water and encasing themselves in mud.

Goldfish seem to have inherited this ability to survive with very little water or oxygen, and tales of goldfish surviving long periods out of water are common.

BREEDING

Wild Crucians and Gibels spawn in the spring, usually between the months of May and July, at a temperature of 15 degrees Celsius (59 degrees Fahrenheit). The fish spawn in shoals, among the water

Beautiful to look at and easy to care for, the goldfish makes an ideal pet for people of all ages and situations.

plants of shallow bays, with each individual female laying up to 250,000 eggs.

In the wild, there are some remarkable all-female populations of Gibel, able to reproduce without males – a process known as parthenogenesis. The eggs hatch and develop into fish fry, but, due to the absence of any male genes, the resulting fry are all female.

Occasionally, some eggs may be fertilised by a male from another species, producing hybrids.

SIZE

The Gibel may reach 12 inches (30 cms) in length. A Crucian may grow even bigger, reaching 20 inches (50 cms). A very large Crucian could weigh as much as 7.5 lbs (3.4 kgs).

LIFESPAN

In the wild, goldfish rarely live for more than six years. In captivity, however, a well-cared-for goldfish may live for up to 30 years. The average age, however, is in the region of 10 years.

PET GOLDFISH

You could argue that the goldfish is undervalued. Some of the more expensive tropical fish – and coldwater fish like the Koi – are seen as more valuable.

Compared to most tropical and coldwater species, goldfish are inexpensive. They are, however, just as colourful. The common goldfish is a splendid example, with its vibrant red/orange colouring, and its beautiful scales.

The goldfish also has a deeper, more mystical side, devotees of Feng Shui giving special attention to the right numbers of goldfish of the right colour, and even suggesting that pet fish can take on the ills of their owners. Goldfish also make ideal pets for those with allergies to animal hair.

Goldfish are hardy pets, and easy to keep. They are happy indoors or out, in a wide variety of temperatures.

Finally, the goldfish will eat almost anything, is happy to share its tank with other species, and is resistant to most diseases.

The goldfish is an important symbol according to Feng Shui tradition.

2 *Goldfish Varieties*

Faced with the picture of an ancestral wild Crucian and one of the more exotic fancy goldfish, it is hard to believe that they are related. Their wildly different appearances are the result of intensive breeding practices, which have exaggerated certain characteristics.

BREEDING PROGRAMMES

When fish are kept in a suitable environment, they will breed. If the fry survive, and breeding continues, mutated fish will eventually be produced. For the goldfish, the first signs of mutation appeared when the captive carp populations of the Orient began to produce gold-coloured individuals.

Once the common goldfish was established, other mutations arose. Strangely shaped fins appeared – sometimes the fins were absent altogether. Other fish were born with a build-up of skin around the head, known as a wen, which gave them the appearance of wearing a hood. Other fish developed

The different varieties of fancy goldfish are the result of intensive breeding programmes.

Common goldfish: Characterised by a long body and bright-red coloration, this is the easiest variety to keep.

deformities around the eyes, had oddly shaped bodies, or grew peculiar-looking scales.

The fish farmers decided that some of these developments were worth 'fixing', i.e. ensuring that the features appeared consistently. The fancy goldfish available today are a result of these intensive breeding programmes.

The different colours seen in the goldfish were also fixed in this way. As well as the traditional red-gold colour, black, chocolate brown, pale orange, yellow, and white also appeared.

COMPLICATIONS
The fixing of these mutations has come at a price. The constricted body shape of most fancies can mean that they are prone to swimbladder problems. Their long fins are easily torn, they often swim slowly, and they have small mouths. This can lead to difficulty in feeding – especially when competing against common goldfish.

Furthermore, fancy goldfish do not cope well with lower temperatures, such as those in a winter pond.

COMMON GOLDFISH
Today's goldfish has an elongated body and bright-red coloration. Elegant in appearance, and extremely easy to keep, it is the ideal fish for the novice.

SHUBUNKIN

There are two main varieties: the London Shubunkin and the Bristol Shubunkin. The London Shubunkin is shaped much like the common goldfish, while the Bristol Shubunkin has much larger fins and a floaty tail. Both varieties are coloured in a mixture of white and orange with blue/black spots or patches – a colour scheme known as calico.

London Shubunkin: Typical calico colouring and shaped like the common goldfish.

Bristol Shubunkin: This variety has longer fins and a more elaborate tail than the London Shubunkin.

GOLDFISH VARIETIES

RYUKIN

The Ryukin has a steep back and a protruding belly, which give it a very rounded appearance.

In motion, the Ryukin is very graceful, its V-shaped tail and paired anal fins contributing to its elegant style of movement.

Ryukin: A rounded fish with elegant fins.

FANTAIL

Similar to the Ryukin, the Fantail takes its name from its fan-shaped tail. Whereas the Ryukin's caudal (tail) fin is more pointed, the Fantail has a shorter and more rounded tail, giving a softer appearance.

This fish also has a more egg-shaped body.

Fantail: Takes its name from its fan-shaped tail.

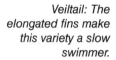

Veiltail: The elongated fins make this variety a slow swimmer.

VEILTAIL

The Veiltail has a long, double-finned tail, which gracefully hangs downwards. This, coupled with elongated anal fins, gives the Veiltail a layered and very attractive appearance at its rear – hence its name.

Although graceful in motion, the Veiltail has a slow swimming technique, and the fishkeeper needs to ensure that this fish gets its fair share of food.

BLACKMOOR

The Moor or Blackmoor is an all-black metallic scaled goldfish, usually with a paired tail and a high dorsal fin. The Blackmoor is often confused with dark-coloured fish of other varieties – e.g. a black 'Blackmoor' with telescopic eyes is actually a black Demekin. To confuse the issue still further, you will see brown fish labelled Chocolate Moor – or black and white 'Panda' Moors.

Blackmoor: This variety is easily recognised by its dramatic black colouring.

Oranda: A short body with a twin tail, this variety comes in different colours.

ORANDA

The Oranda has a shortened, full-bodied appearance, with a twin tail and an elongated dorsal fin (i.e. the fin on top of the fish's back), which distinguishes it from its similar-looking cousin, the Lionhead. The Oranda's defining characteristic is the wen around its head. The Oranda comes in a variety of colours.

LIONHEAD

This fish seems to send the Japanese experts into raptures. With its neat, tapered body, absent dorsal fin and its short, neat, twin tail, it is an attractive fish that comes in several colours.

Like the Oranda, the Lionhead's cauliflower-shaped wen leaves only the eyes and mouth uncovered.

Lionhead: A short, neat-looking fish, notable for the absence of its dorsal fin.

BUBBLE EYE

It is not difficult to see how the Bubble Eye acquired its name. Large lymph-filled bubbles sit under each eye. These bags are easily torn or damaged, so the fishkeeper must make sure there are no sharp or abrasive objects in the aquarium.

As with many other fancy goldfish, the Bubble Eye is a slow swimmer.

YOSAKIN

Yosakins can be divided into Demekins and Tosakins. The Demekin can be distinguished from the Tosakin because of its protruding telescopic eyes.

When swimming, the Tosakin's tail looks very much like a flapping butterfly. This effect is the result of two tails that are joined at the base. Unfortunately, it also reduces the Tosakin's grace in the water.

PEARLSCALE

The Pearlscale's name derives from the translucent quality of its white colour. This fish bears a striking resemblance to a golf ball. It has a rounded body, covered with raised, domed scales, and a rounded fan-shaped tail.

RANCHU

The Ranchu is a strange-looking goldfish, with a seemingly misshapen body.

The down-turned tail extends right into the body, giving the spine a bent appearance.

Bubble Eye: Large, lymph-filled bubbles are situated under each eye.

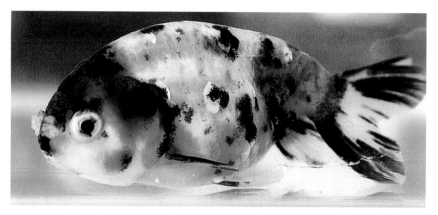

Pompom: 'Cheerleader' pompoms are located above each nostril.

POMPOM

The Pompom is one of the easiest goldfish varieties to identify. It has very distinctive 'nasal bouquets' – skin growths which resemble a cheerleader's pompoms – one above each nostril.

Like most goldfish varieties, the Pompom comes in different colours.

CELESTIAL

The Celestial is a twin-tailed goldfish, not unlike the Ryukin (see page 15). It has protruding eyes upturned on the top of its head. This feature leaves the Celestial gazing permanently at the stars, making feeding very difficult if it is surrounded by livelier fish.

3 *Aquarium Equipment*

Buying aquarium equipment can be a daunting experience, as there is a bewildering array of products available.

You may see small tanks containing basic equipment, advertised as a complete system for goldfish. Many of these are too small for all but a tiny, single goldfish.

Larger tanks, with built-in filtration and lights, are often ideal for goldfish and may provide a quick and easy entry into fishkeeping. However, goldfish can be kept healthy and happy with a minimum of equipment.

So, before you buy any equipment, you should consider your bank balance and the size of your home. Aquarium equipment is no more expensive than the

equipment used in many other hobbies, but, for a large, well-equipped aquarium, you should expect to spend a reasonable amount of money.

TANKS

Before you buy an aquarium, take a look around your home. Do you have the space for a decent-sized tank, and, if so, where are you going to put it?

SIZE

The standard aquarium is rectangular, available in lengths of 2 feet (61 cms), 3 feet (91 cms) or 4 feet (122 cms), with widths of 12 inches (31 cms), 18 inches (46 cms) or 2 feet (61 cms). You do not have to choose the biggest aquarium in the shop, but you should choose the largest you can afford. Some novices keep two or three young goldfish very successfully in a 2-foot (61-cm) tank, but this is the minimum size you should consider.

Ideally, your aquarium should be big enough to house six or more fish, because goldfish are only really happy in shoals. Each goldfish is likely to reach 4 inches (10 cms) in length – some grow far larger – and your choice of aquarium must reflect this.

A good pet shop will be happy to advise you about which aquarium is the best. Small starter tanks are better stocked with small, 'easy-care' tropical fish, such as the White Cloud Mountain minnow.

ACRYLIC OR GLASS?

Until recently, glass aquariums were the only type available. However, many shops now sell acrylic tanks.

The main advantage of an acrylic aquarium is that it is virtually indestructible. The main drawback is the price. Generally, acrylic is a more expensive option than glass. It also scratches more easily, spoiling your view of the fish. Acrylic tanks are more difficult to clean than glass ones, because of their tendency to become scratched. Dirt and algae can build up in deep scratches, and are difficult to remove. Scratching, however, can be kept to a minimum by careful cleaning. Choose a pad suitable for acrylic and avoid getting grit on it.

If you decide to opt for the traditional glass aquarium, check the thickness of the glass. Some tanks are made of extremely thin glass, and the pressure created by filling the tank can lead to fractures or breakage. In the UK, the

Ornamental Aquatic Trade Association have set standards for glass thickness. Look for their logo before agreeing to buy a glass aquarium.

ALTERNATIVE SHAPES

Whatever shape of tank you want, it is likely to exist. Do not forfeit function for style, however; the most important consideration is the welfare of your fish.

Tanks designed to fit into corners can be very helpful and space-saving. Hexagonal and other narrow, column-shaped tanks should be avoided.

The goldfish is a browsing fish, which means it is happiest towards the bottom of the tank, exploring a large area of substrate (i.e. the gravel covering the bottom of the tank). Hexagonal and column-shaped tanks are taller than they are wide, giving the goldfish limited space on the substrate. Very tall column tanks are also very difficult to clean properly.

A corner tank is an excellent space saver. Column tanks offer limited space at the base.

HOODS AND STANDS

When you buy your aquarium, you should also buy a hood (the 'lid' of the tank) and a stand. Some aquariums will be sold with these items included.

HOODS

If possible, opt for a hood which has water-resistant or waterproof light fittings built in. These are more expensive than the plain hoods, but are safer and better suited to the new fishkeeper.

You should also check that the hood has holes at the back for the necessary cables and airline to pass through. Some hoods also offer dedicated spaces for fluorescent-lighting starters, air pumps and other equipment.

STANDS

When full, even the smallest aquarium will be too heavy for most standard furniture. Tank stands are reinforced to hold the weight of a full tank, and some of the basic ones, which can hold just as much weight as the more elaborate types, are relatively inexpensive.

Some aquarium stands look like high-quality pieces of furniture, complete with cupboard doors. The space below the tank can be

Some tanks come complete with their own cabinet.

used to house your aquarium equipment and fishfood, holding all the unattractive but necessary items of fishkeeping equipment.

HEATERS

Goldfish are hardy creatures, and commons will not require a heated tank. Fancy goldfish will need extra heat only if the tank is situated in a cold place.

If you install a heater, you should never heat the water beyond 24 degrees Celsius (75 degrees Fahrenheit). High

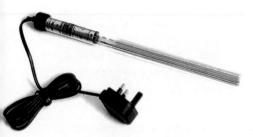

If you are keeping fancy goldfish, you may need to provide heating.

A thermometer means you can keep a check on temperature.

temperatures are far more dangerous to goldfish than lower ones. During the summer, an aquarium can easily reach temperatures of around 27 degrees Celsius (80 degrees Fahrenheit), which reduces the oxygen content in the water.

Tropical fish may be equipped to deal with this, but even the hardiest goldfish may not be able to obtain sufficient oxygen from the water passing over its gills.

A thermometer is a cheap and simple piece of equipment that will help you to maintain a constant temperature in your aquarium. Your pet store will sell several varieties, including the simple stick-on form, and the more complex glass type.

Digital thermometers are now available at a reasonable price, and can be purchased from your pet store or local pharmacy.

LIGHTS

Goldfish have no actual requirement for light. If your tank receives sufficient natural daylight for you to see your fish, you may never want to purchase a light.

Aquarium lights come in a range of sizes and colours, and many goldfish owners purchase them to create lighting effects. Your local aquatic pet specialists will be happy to advise you on a suitable light for this.

If you use an aquarium light, try to emulate natural patterns of sunlight, leaving the light on for 8 to 12 hours a day.

AIRPUMPS

Airpumps are a multi-purpose piece of equipment, and every aquarium owner should have one. The main function of the airpump

An airpump adds oxygen to the water.

is to add oxygen to the water, but it can also be used to power both everyday filtration systems, and emergency filtration (see page 49).

The most common types of airpump have a vibrating arm controlled by an electromagnet, which pulls a diaphragm in and out to pump air through a one-way valve. They are generally used in conjunction with an airstone (a porous 'rock' which distributes the air), which is attached to an airline leading from the airpump.

FILTERS

Filters are needed to complete the nitrogen cycle, a process which takes place everywhere on the planet. All plants and animals contain protein. When living things die, the proteins break down, producing ammonia. In your fish tank, ammonia is produced by rotting fishfood, decaying plants and fish excrement. Ammonia is very harmful to fish, and will kill them if levels rise too high.

Aquarium filters have a dual role. All filters contain some form of filtration media, and water is either pumped, sucked or otherwise drawn through and around this media. In many cases, this media consists of a piece of sponge.

As the water is drawn through the sponge, particles of waste are removed, a process known as mechanical filtration. A sponge has lots of surfaces, and oxygen-

Filtration is a necessary process in a healthy aquarium.

loving, aerobic bacteria sit on these surfaces, using oxygen to break down ammonia to nitrite – a process usually called biological filtration.

Unfortunately, nitrites are highly toxic, and are as deadly to fish as ammonia. Fortunately, other aerobic bacteria break down the nitrites, converting them to nitrates, which, at normal levels, are relatively harmless.

To complete the cycle, anaerobic bacteria can be cultured in a filter with a very low oxygen supply, to break down nitrates. However, this is a much more complex process. Instead, goldfish keepers make regular water changes to dilute the nitrates.

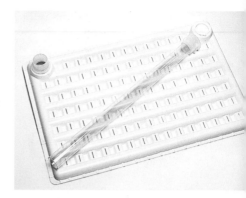

The gravel substrate acts as a filter in an undergravel filter.

CHOOSING A FILTER

There are many different types of filter. Both the common, and some of the more advanced, methods of filtration are covered in this chapter. Your choice of filter should be based on the size of your aquarium, the number of fish you keep, and your personal budget.

UNDERGRAVEL FILTERS

The undergravel filter is a traditional and very effective means of cleaning the water in your aquarium. It works by making the gravel substrate act as the filter.

A perforated plate is positioned in the bottom of the tank. Attached to the plate are one or more tubes, called uplifts, which reach towards the surface of the water. The plate is covered with 3 inches (7 cms) of gravel, and water is sucked or pushed up the uplifts, drawing the main body of water down through the gravel substrate.

The gravel traps any solid matter (and must therefore be cleaned regularly), and aerobic bacteria fix to the surfaces of the gravel, turning the whole substrate into a filter.

There are several ways of setting up an undergravel filter. An airstone can be placed in the uplift pipe(s). As the bubbles rise in the uplift, they carry water with them and more water oozes in through the gravel.

Alternatively, a small pump, called a powerhead, can be placed on top of the uplift. This actively pumps the water through the pipe.

Some powerheads allow you to pump water down the pipe, known as 'reverse-flow' filtration. This method pushes some of the wastes clear of the gravel and may help to keep the gravel cleaner.

INTERNAL FILTERS

As the name suggests, internal filters are placed inside the aquarium. They are powered in various ways.

A simple 'bubble-up' filter uses a similar method to an air-powered undergravel filter, in which rising bubbles draw water through a box of filter media of your choice.

Most common is the simple, electrically-powered internal filter, which consists of a pump on top of a slatted box, usually containing a sponge medium.

A comparatively recent innovation are internal filters with several compartments. These offer mechanical, biological and even

The internal filter is fitted inside the tank.

chemical filtration. In chemical filtration, the medium is usually carbon or a resin, capable of removing harmful chemicals from the water.

Basic internal filters are probably the best option for the goldfish keeper. They are less expensive and easier to maintain than the more sophisticated external filters, and can be bought in a range of sizes to suit the popular aquarium sizes.

For smaller tanks, an air-powered bubble-up filter can work well. It offers gentle filtration with few turbulent currents. For everyday fishkeeping, the ordinary electric-pump-powered internal filter containing a sponge will filter a goldfish tank comfortably.

The more sophisticated systems are extremely effective but can be expensive to run. Some parts, such as the chemical filter pads and disposable pre-filters, will need to be replaced regularly.

EXTERNAL FILTERS

The external filter is popular and widely used, particularly in the UK. It consists of a bucket filled with filter media, through which water is pumped.

The filter is placed below the tank, and has a pump which pushes water back up to the tank. To work, this pump needs to be primed, and several modern external filters allow you to do this simply. Otherwise, you will have to suck on the pipes to begin the siphoning of water down to the bucket.

Once in the bucket, the water percolates through the filter media and is then pumped back to the tank. All the water in the tank should pass through the filter approximately once every hour.

The filter media may vary, but most filters contain more than one form. A typical arrangement might include:

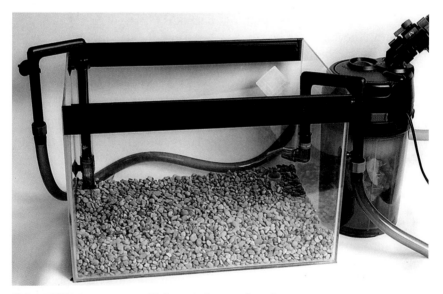

External filters can cope with large volumes of waste.

- A polishing medium like floss to remove even the finest particles of waste.
- A sponge, with a large surface area for helpful bacteria, which removes solid waste.
- A medium with a large surface area of ceramic, plastic or sintered glass (i.e. glass which has been baked to create a porous surface), in which yet more helpful aerobic bacteria build up.

External filters tend to be popular because they can cope with large amounts of waste, and are adaptable, allowing temporary media to be added to the filter to combat a specific water pollutant. For example, carbon can be added to the filter to remove water discoloration and poisonous chemicals.

HANG-ON FILTERS

Hang-on filters are very popular in the US but not easy to buy in the UK. The filter hangs on the side of the tank – hence the name. Water is pumped out of the tank and through the filter media, re-entering though a weir system that oxygenates the water.

FLUIDISED BED FILTERS

Fluidised bed filters consist of a container of liquidised sand. The sand is churned around constantly, by pumping water from the aquarium through the filter. Each grain of sand grinds away against the others, which, in turn, grinds away dirt and dead bacteria cells. This leaves a perfect surface on which the live bacteria can live, constantly exposed to the water, and so able to help break down ammonia and nitrites.

Fluidised bed filters offer excellent filtration. Such a filter can also be complicated to set up and maintain, as flow rates must be exactly right or the sand will clog. Those new to fishkeeping would be better choosing a simpler filtration method.

TRICKLE FILTERS

Trickle filters are commonly used in marine fishkeeping and with large freshwater tropical fish, but they can also be used for goldfish. Water is pumped out of the tank to trickle over filter media with a large surface area. The filter media is exposed to the air, offering the vital aerobic bacteria ideal conditions in which to function.

4 *Setting Up Your Aquarium*

Thorough planning is required when planning a successful goldfish aquarium. Be clear about the location of your aquarium, and the sort of set-up you want, before moving a single piece of equipment.

POSITIONING YOUR AQUARIUM

The position of your aquarium is very important. Take the following factors into account:
• Peace and quiet for your goldfish
• A strong, stable floor surface
• Easy access to water and electrical supplies.

CHOOSING A ROOM

Most people like their goldfish to be in the main room of the house, such as a living room. If you choose a much-used room, make sure your fish have some freedom from over-attentive glass-tapping humans. Noisy or excessively busy locations will make your goldfish stressed and unhappy.

Kitchens are not ideal for aquaria. Cooking vapours and other fumes are potentially lethal to goldfish, and could get into the tank even through the airpump. Bathrooms are also unsuitable because of temperature fluctuations and the lack of a suitable electrical supply.

Whichever room you choose, avoid windows and radiators. Excessive sunshine promotes algae growth, while the heat from radiators will increase the temperature in the tank.

Remember to choose a position which is near an electrical socket, and allows you an easy passage to a sink or taps. You will need a strong, level floor, capable of coping with a water-filled aquarium, which, for a standard 8 feet^3 (2x2x2) tank alone is 50 UK gallons/60 US fluid gallons (227 litres), which weighs approximately 500 lbs (227 kg).

Your goldfish will appreciate being located away from the hurly-burly of the household.

ASSEMBLY

Position your chosen stand, making sure you can easily reach the electrical supply point. Some aquaria need a layer of polystyrene placed under them but this is rare these days. Position the tank on the stand, and make sure that the hood fits and allows access for all the equipment you have chosen to use.

The stand or cabinet may offer a cupboard suitable for an external filter, and in which other equipment, all the wires, and a cable tidy can be concealed.

With the hood off the tank, add the substrate (if using an undergravel filter, position the plate and the uplifts first), and then start positioning the other equipment.

FILTER SET-UPS

Goldfish will adapt to a wide range of tank set-ups. Here are four suggested filtration methods.

LOW-TECH

If you have plenty of spare time, you can keep your goldfish using little more than a tank and a plentiful supply of good-quality water. You will not need a filter in this low-tech aquarium. Instead, you must perform water changes of up to 20-30 per cent, two to three times a week (see page 47).

If you choose the low-tech set-up, you must maintain a low

stocking level. In a tank of 3 feet x 15 inches x 15 inches (1 metre x 40 cms x 40 cms), you can keep no more than three or four goldfish, each of 2 inches or 3 inches (5 cms or 7.5 cms) in length. Stick to a sensible feeding regime – if you decide to indulge your fish with some extra food, there will be no filter to remove the harmful ammonia which will be produced when it is digested or decays.

STANDARD UNDERGRAVEL

In a small- to medium-sized tank, the standard undergravel set-up is ideal. Fit the correct size of undergravel plate, and cover it with three to four inches of gravel.

The undergravel plate should be covered with 3-4 ins of gravel.

Power it using a powerhead or powerheads, or with airstones in the uplift(s).

To help the gravel substrate stay clean, you can back up the undergravel using a small internal power filter. This will remove some wastes while they are still suspended in the water.

It is possible to have the filtering gravel separate from the rest of the substrate. Create a channel at the rear of the aquarium, by siliconing in a piece of glass the same length as your tank and about 6 inches high. Fit the plates and uplifts in this area, covering them with a 5-inch-thick layer of gravel. The rest of the aquarium base can be covered with either a finer layer of gravel or another more specialised substrate – perhaps one suitable for growing plants.

DOUBLE INTERNAL FILTER

This set-up is ideal for medium-sized tanks. Purchase two internal power filters, each able to cope with a tank just over half the size of yours. For example, if you had a 4-foot (1.2-metre) tank, you should purchase filters which are designed to cope with 3 feet (0.9 metres) individually. Place one filter at either end of the tank.

Internal filters should be placed at either end of the tank.

One of the filters should be cleaned every two weeks, so that each filter is cleaned monthly. This means that you always have a mature filter with a good head of helpful bacteria. As you should wash the sponge media supplied in tank water only, make filter-cleaning part of your water-change regime.

EXTERNAL FILTER

External filters are the best choice for anyone who wishes to maintain a large, heavily-stocked aquarium, i.e. anything over 4 feet (1.2 metres).

A good-quality external filter may contain a sponge filter, a compartment containing sintered glass, and some filter floss to give

a final polish. I always like to have room to add a bag of carbon or ammonia-removing resin in emergencies.

One of the drawbacks to the external set-up is that it can injure fancy goldfish varieties. As water is sucked up the filter's intake pipes, the flowing and delicate fins of some varieties can be drawn into the pipe, even through the cage-like covers.

External filters can be set up to return the water through a spraybar – a length of plastic pipe with a line of regularly spaced holes along one side – which splashes water onto the surface. The spraybar can create currents that sensitive fancies may dislike. Many experienced fishkeepers prefer to use a short length of plastic pipe to steer the flow into one corner of the tank and so limit the current.

COMBINATIONS

For high-quality filtration with minimal maintenance, purchase a medium-sized internal filter and an external filter, and run them together. The internal filter removes the suspended wastes in the water, which are a lot easier to remove from its sponge than from deep inside the external filter.

FITTING THE AIRPUMP

Airpumps are not waterproof and are designed for use outside the tank. Even then they should always be positioned above the water line. If they are below the water level, and the pump switches off unexpectedly (e.g. during a power cut), it is possible for water to back-siphon down the airline and into the pump. The airpump will flood, and, when power is restored, electricity and water will meet in a potentially lethal combination. At best, the pump will short out and never work again.

Some airpumps are supplied with a non-return valve (or they can be bought separately). Fitted into the airline, the valve stops water back-siphoning, but may reduce the amount of air pumped through, placing an extra strain on the airpump's diaphragm.

FITTING THE LIGHTS

Most goldfish keepers will opt for fluorescent lighting using one or two tubes. Each fluorescent light tube will need a starter to control it and these are bulky.

Some modern aquarium hoods have these built in. If not, you must decide whether the starters will fit in the hood, can be hung

Lighting can be fitted into the tank hood.

on the back of the cabinet (you will probably have to position a screw or hook eye), or will be placed in the cabinet itself (presuming the wires will stretch – which they often do not).

Fluorescent tubes fit into endcaps which are wired into the starter. In the better, newer systems, these have been made near-watertight, which adds an extra degree of safety to the tank.

USING A CABLE TIDY

Most of the equipment described is electrical, but plugging in three or four plugs per tank is awkward. The solution is a cable tidy – all the equipment can be wired into this, and most models have switches that allow you to switch lights, filters or airpumps on and off separately. Just one cable feeds the cable tidy, so only one plug and socket are required.

TANK DECOR

Once you have assembled your aquarium and installed the equipment, you are ready to decorate. The only limit is your imagination.

BACKGROUNDS

Goldfish look magnificent against a black or dark-blue background. To achieve this effect you can either paint the tank (on the outside), or glue on paper or other coloured material. Alternatively, most pet shops sell specialist aquaria backdrops, which come in a variety of colours and designs.

CHOOSING A SUBSTRATE

There are various forms of substrate available, all of which should be purchased from aquatic stores, where the substrates are known to be safe.

GRAVEL

The most popular choice of substrate is gravel. This comes in a variety of sizes and colours.

Gravel substrates can trap a lot

Gravel should be washed thoroughly before using it in the aquarium.

of dirt. This is less of a problem with goldfish as they love to suck at the individual grains, doing a lot of the necessary cleaning for you. There must be no sharp edges on the gravel, or your goldfish may injure themselves.

Thoroughly wash the gravel before adding it to the tank.

SAND

Sand is not an ideal substrate for goldfish. While searching for food, the fish disturb the sand and churn it up. It will cloud the water and clog the filters.

Sand can also be dangerous if it is undisturbed. The areas of sand that manage to escape your goldfish's attention may harbour anaerobic bacteria, which produce poisonous hydrogen sulphide.

A popular alternative, which looks similar to sand, is sealed grit. Sealed grit consists of tiny pieces of coloured gravel slightly larger than sand. This coated grit is much cleaner than sand and, once rinsed, has no fine, dusty bits to cloud the water.

PLANTING MEDIA

Planting media is never used as a complete substrate – it must be placed underneath a top layer of gravel if you use it to grow aquatic plants.

Never use horticultural products in an aquarium. Instead, use either one of the many planting media sold for tropical planted aquaria, or the soil sold for potting pond plants.

ROCKS

As with gravel, make sure that there are no sharp edges on your rocks, and be sure to buy them from a pet store. Rocks sold for aquatic use are inert and should not have any effect on the water chemistry, whereas rocks taken from the beach or your garden may harm your fish.

As a very rough rule of thumb, dark-coloured rocks, such as flint or slate, are safest. Pale rocks may have high levels of calcium which could make the water dangerously hard.

BOGWOOD

Bogwood is a general term applied to all the varieties of wood commonly used in aquaria. It comes in all shapes and sizes, and not just from bogs...

Bogwood can add interest to your aquarium, but only use wood intended for use in aquaria, and be sure to check your pH levels regularly (see page 40). Bogwood may lower the pH levels in aquaria, making the water more acidic.

Nearly all varieties of bogwood will dye your aquarium water. This has no detrimental effect on the fish, and most of the time the leaching is barely noticeable.

Make sure the rocks have no sharp edges.

In some cases, the slightly brown tinge produced by some bogwood may contribute favourably to the look of the aquarium. If you find the colouring overpowering, the dye can be removed by adding carbon to your filter.

After purchasing bogwood, it will need to be thoroughly cleaned and soaked before you can add it to your tank. Clean it with a new, clean scrubbing brush.

Next, place the bogwood in a bowl or bucket, and leave it to soak. Once it has absorbed enough water to sink to the bottom of the bucket, it is ready to add to your aquarium.

Some wood will sink immediately, but it should be left in the bucket for a while, allowing a little more of the yellow colour to be leached from the bogwood. Occasionally, you may need to help the sinking process by letting the wood dry then siliconing a rock or other weight to the wood to make it sink.

AQUARIUM PLANTS
The main choice is between plastic plants or live plants.

Of the live plants, *Vallisneria*, also known as Vallis, is perhaps the best known. *Vallisneria spiralis* copes well with temperatures down to 15 degrees Celsius (59

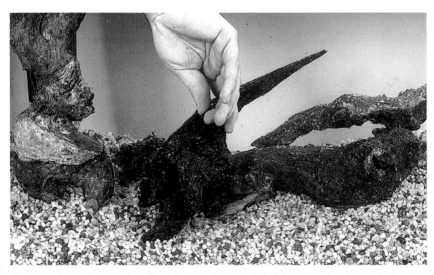

Bogwood creates a natural-looking environment, but keep a check on pH levels.

degrees Fahrenheit), and requires little light.

Plants which look similar to plants growing in natural environments are the leggy *Egeria* and *Echinodorus* plants. *Echinodorus bleheri*, although better suited to temperatures higher than 20 degrees Celsius (68 degrees Fahrenheit), can look fantastic.

A more adaptable plant is the red-speckled *Echinodorus* 'Ozelot', which is comfortable in temperatures down to 15 degrees Celsius (59 degrees Fahrenheit). This plant may send striking runners to the water surface.

An easy-to-cultivate plant is the Java fern *(Microsorum pteropus)*.

This plant needs only to be tied to a rock or a piece of bogwood. It does, however, prefer temperatures over 18 degrees Celsius (64 degrees Fahrenheit).

To grow natural plants really successfully you need (at the very least) good lighting and a proper planting medium.

PLASTIC IDEAS
Many fishkeepers find that their goldfish nibble the aquarium plants, quickly making them appear bedraggled. Others find natural plants very difficult to grow.

To overcome these problems, many goldfish owners use plastic

You will need to have good lighting for plants to thrive.

plants. You can have lots of fun choosing different colour combinations to decorate your tank – just use your imagination.

ESTABLISHING YOUR AQUARIUM

The most important component of a healthy aquarium is high-quality water. (See page 42 for how to establish a successful fish community.)

WATER QUALITY

Goldfish are more resistant to natural pollution than most fish, but poor-quality tapwater puts any fish under increased stress. This puts the goldfish at a higher risk of developing an infection or contracting a parasite infestation.

Tapwater can contain chlorine and chloramine, both of which are unpleasant or potentially harmful to your fish. Tapwater may also contain high levels of nitrates and phosphates (which encourage algae growths), and, occasionally, nastier things like pesticides. As a result, it pays to prepare the water you use for your tank in advance.

A simple chemical pod attached to a hose from your tap, or a more complicated tapwater filter, can be used to pre-filter your tapwater. If using a tapwater filter, it must be suitable for use in fishkeeping – domestic tapwater filters are not.

As an alternative, you could use several white buckets, such as those suitable for home brewing or food use. These can be used to store water while it is treated with carbon- or nitrate-removing resin in an air-powered bubble-up filter.

CHEMICALS

Most fishkeepers use a bottled chemical dechlorinator when preparing fresh water for their aquarium. Some enthusiasts argue that it is unnecessary, and that simply leaving water to stand, or aerating it thoroughly beforehand, disperses any chlorine.

This is true, but it does not take the problem of chloramine into account. Chloramine is chlorine with ammonia added to stabilise it

A bottled chemical dechlorinator will prepare tapwater so it is suitable for your fish.

while it removes harmful bacteria from your drinking water supply.

When you remove the chlorine, the ammonia remains. So, when using untreated tapwater, use a dechlorinator that removes chlorine and locks up any ammonia every time you make a water change.

WATER TESTING

The simplest way to check water quality, once your tank has been set up, is to perform a series of tests; namely for ammonia, nitrites, and pH level (water acidity). These tests should be performed once a week. Simple test kits can be bought at every aquatic store.

TEMPERATURE

When you perform water changes, the fresh water should be the same temperature as the aquarium water. Adding water which is significantly colder or warmer may send the fish into shock, and it will certainly distress them.

Most goldfish are kept without a heater, so giving stored water time to reach room temperature is all that is required.

FILLING THE TANK

Once all your tank décor is in place in your aquarium, you will not wish to batter it with water and knock it crooked or disturb the gravel, etc.

The best way to add the water is

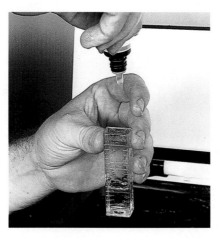
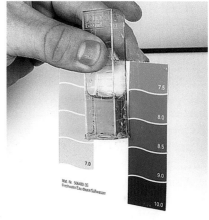

A test kit is easy to use, and you can ensure that your water quality is correct.

from a hose or from a watering can (you can use a rose on the spout to lessen the water pressure), and there are various ways of cushioning the tank decor. Positioning a plate or a colander over the gravel, and pouring the water onto that, works very well.

If you are planting real plants, stop when you have half filled the tank, and do your planting then, before very gently filling the aquarium to the required level.

Once you have filled your tank with water for the first time, use a siphon hose to remove a full bucket of water. The standard 5-UK-gallon/6 US-fluid-gallon (22.75 litre) brewing-bucket is a useful size for performing water changes in a 15 to 25-UK-gallon/18 to 30-US-gallon (68 to 114 litre) aquarium.

Make a small mark on the tank to note this new water level. Then, if you wish, each time you make a water change you can siphon off the aquarium water, straight to waste, until the water level is equal to your mark.

When you add the water, use a bowl so that you do not disturb the substrate.

5 Caring For Your Goldfish

This chapter will guide you through the process of stocking your fish tank, caring for your fish, and maintaining a well-cared-for aquarium.

ESTABLISHING A FISH COMMUNITY

Goldfish are a shoaling species, and should be kept in groups of six or more – a lone goldfish is an unhappy goldfish. However, the fish should not be introduced all at the same time.

When you first establish your aquarium, it will need only a few days to settle down, but it could be six weeks before the filter is biologically mature enough to support a growing stock of goldfish.

You can be certain that everything is working in your tank, and that any live plants will have had a brief chance to establish, about three days after the tank has been filled. At this stage, add two goldfish only. After a further six weeks, if your tests for ammonia and nitrite are clear, add another two fish. Wait another six weeks, do your tests, and then add two more fish.

Continue with this process until your tank has reached its maximum stocking level. This assumes that you are adding small, young fish. Remember that larger goldfish will place more pressure on your filtration.

STOCKING LEVELS

Authorities disagree about the stocking level for goldfish. Goldfish are hardy shoaling fish, and most people believe that six fish (or more) constitute a shoal. On the other hand, goldfish can reach 12 inches (30 cms) or longer, and, in the average aquarium, even a single fish of that size might be a problem. If you keep them well, your goldfish will grow, so you need to allow

RELEASING THE FISH

1. Your fish will be transported home in a polythene bag which should then be allowed to float in the matured tank.

2. Allow the temperature in the bag and the tank to equalise.

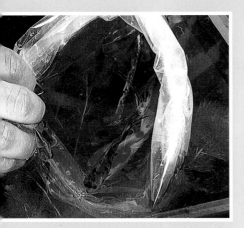

3. Undo the bag, and allow the fish to swim out.

4. The fish will be stressed by their experience, and may lurk at the bottom of the tank to begin with.

If you are keeping fancy varieties, such as the Bubble Eye, do not mix them with Shubunkins or the common goldfish.

them space to grow into.

Here is a helpful rule of thumb to enable you to work out the stocking level for your tank. Multiply the length of the tank by its width. Divide the total by 30 if your measurements are in inches, or 80 if using centimetres. In a 36 x 18-inch (91 x 46-cm) aquarium, the answer would be 21.6 inches (55 cms), which is the total inches of fish which you can stock. In other words, the length of each fish added together (ignore their tails) should not exceed 21.6 inches (55 cms).

Always remember that this is the maximum stocking level. If you are close to reaching it, you will need to ensure that you have adequate filtration, perform regular water changes, and plan for a larger aquarium in the future.

STOCKING DIFFERENT VARIETIES

Your goldfish aquarium does not have to consist of fish all of the same variety. However, great care needs to be taken if you want to mix them.

Never mix commons or Shubunkins with the fancy varieties. Fancies are slow-moving and will be unhappy if kept with the quicker, more boisterous commons. Fancy goldfish varieties also tend to miss out at mealtimes, and may even be molested by the hardier varieties.

Common goldfish seem unable

to resist nipping the fins and tails of the more vulnerable fancies, and I have encountered a case where one goldfish successfully attempted to suck out another's eye!

Goldfish are a species of carp, and some fishkeepers mistakenly believe that goldfish can share an aquarium with other species of carp. This is not the case. Most other species of carp (Common carp, Grass carp, or Tench, for instance) can be kept in a tank only while they are very young. They quickly outgrow aquaria and need to graduate to a pond.

It is also worth remembering that many carp species (e.g. Bream, Dace and Roach) have higher oxygen demands than the goldfish.

Although fancy goldfish can happily cohabit with some varieties of tropical fish, there is a risk of cross-infection. Each is presented with diseases they would not normally encounter. The higher temperatures may not suit the goldfish, and the diseases that they carry and resist at lower temperatures can run riot.

So what can you keep? Weather Loaches make an interesting, eel-like addition to a goldfish tank. Mixing goldfish with Bitterling is another combination, but the latter can occasionally display aggression.

A successful combination is goldfish mixed with a small shoal of minnows. White Cloud Mountain minnows, or Fat Head minnows (also called Rosy Red or

The Weather Loach makes an interesting addition to a goldfish aquarium.

Goldfish need to be provided with a well-balanced diet.

Golden minnows) are the best choice. Occasionally, a larger goldfish may eat a White Cloud Mountain minnow, but the larger Fat Heads should not be at risk.

FEEDING

Goldfish are omnivorous. Wild or pond-dwelling goldfish would survive on midge larvae, water hoglice, shrimps, aquatic worms, small snails and other molluscs. They would also ingest large amounts of algae and weed.

Apart from algae, aquarium goldfish have no naturally occurring food, so it is the responsibility of the fishkeeper to provide their goldfish with a varied and well-balanced diet.

FLAKES AND PELLETS

The bulk of your goldfish food can consist of fresh, high-quality flake, granule or pellet food from your aquatic dealer. These will supply your goldfish with all the nutrients they need.

However, processed foods are the main suspect in some of the digestive problems suffered by fancy goldfish, and fish will quickly become bored with such a basic diet, so supplement it with other foods once or twice a week.

OTHER FOODS

Goldfish have very wide-ranging tastes, and will appreciate some blanched vegetables, such as broccoli or fresh cucumber slices.

Meaty foods, like earthworms or frozen irradiated bloodworm or shrimp, will also be eaten with relish.

If you give earthworms to your goldfish, make sure you observe them being eaten. A missed earthworm will crawl into the gravel and, once it dies, can be a hidden source of pollution.

OVERFEEDING

The instructions on most goldfish foods recommend feeding your fish two or three times a day. This may not be necessary, and may even be detrimental to your fishes' health.

Goldfish will not stop eating, even when they have had more than enough. Any food consumed beyond what is necessary is excreted back into the water, undigested, which rapidly increases the levels of ammonia in the water.

Likewise, if you give your fish too much food, some of it will sink to the bottom of the tank, where it will decompose and pollute the water. The rising ammonia levels make it harder for your filter to maintain good water quality, and toxins can reach fatal levels in a surprisingly short time.

FEEDING PRACTICES

Only feed your fish once a day – twice at most. Choose a time when you can stay near the tank and get a chance to observe your fish. Make sure that all the food is gone in ten minutes and that each fish is getting enough to eat. Perform a quick head count, and take a close look to ensure that all your fish are in good health.

WATER CHANGES

To keep your fish healthy, you need to change part of the aquarium water at regular

Regular, partial water changes are needed to keep your fish healthy.

intervals. This will prevent pollution levels from rising too high and damaging your fish.

Water changes are made using a siphon hose, which siphons off the water into a bucket. A bucket which contains 5 UK gal/6 US fl gal (22.7 litres), is a good guideline for how much water you should remove and replace in a regular water change (see individual tank set-ups, below, for how often this should be done).

Each time you prepare to change the water, do not forget to treat the new water (at the very least using a dechlorinator), so that it is safe for your fish.

LOW-TECH TANKS
It is possible to run an aquarium for goldfish with no filtration – just like the traditional goldfish bowl but much, much larger. In this set-up, water changes should be made two or three times a week.

For a standard-sized aquarium, for example, a 3-foot tank (i.e. 3 feet x 12 inches x 15 inches/1 metre x 30 cms x 40 cms), you will need to replace 5 UK gal/6 US fl gal (23 litres) of the full-capacity 20 UK gal/24 US fl gal (91 litres), with every water change.

The percentage of water you change will largely depend on the stocking level in your aquarium. It may be necessary to change up to 50 per cent of the water if your tank is particularly heavily stocked. In some ways, you are swapping the time spent changing water for the cost of more sophisticated equipment.

UNDERGRAVEL FILTER TANKS
Tanks which are filtered using an undergravel filter need water changes approximately once every two weeks. Each time a water change is made, 30 per cent of the water should be replaced.

You should also regularly clean the gravel, as it will contain lots of mulm from wastes filtered out from the aquarium and broken down by the filter bacteria (see page 51).

DOUBLE INTERNAL FILTER TANKS
The double internal filter set-up requires a water change every two weeks. Roughly 30 per cent of the water should be changed, although the percentage will vary according to how intensively stocked your tank is.

Each time a water change is made, just one of the filters should

Test your water regularly to ensure that pollutants do not build up.

be cleaned out using the tank water.

EXTERNAL FILTER TANKS

The external filter is one of the most effective forms of filtration. Consequently, a water change may be required only once a month; if water tests reveal a high level of pollutants, however, you should perform an interim water change. Between 30 per cent and 50 per cent of the water should be changed, depending on stocking levels.

EMERGENCY WATER CHANGES

Despite regular water changes, you may find your fish becoming ill, or a test may reveal a dangerous level of pollutants. Specific water tests or a close examination of your filter may reveal the nature of the problem, but take no chances. Make an emergency water change and/or add extra filtration immediately.

Very often, high levels of ammonia are the cause of the problem. Ammonia-removing resins, such as zeolite, are very good as an interim solution to this problem. Add zeolite in a bubble-up filter powered by your airpump and airstone.

Mystery problems can sometimes be alleviated by carbon used in the same way. Carbon will not remove ammonia or nitrite but is effective against many other forms of pollution.

In warm weather, in very dirty tanks, or when medicating fish, lack of oxygen can be a problem. While you are trying to diagnose the specific problem, use your airpump to add extra oxygen to the water.

Emergency treatments, such as carbon or zeolite, should always be accompanied by a substantial water change. In an ideal world, you should always have a bucket of fresh, treated, replacement water in storage. It can, of course, be used for your regular water changes, if not needed for an emergency.

A variety of tank cleaners is available.

Remember to replace this emergency supply regularly, so that the water is always ready.

CLEANING THE AQUARIUM

Regular water changes should be supported by good aquarium hygiene. Regular cleaning of the tank and its apparatus should be done each time you change the water. Filter media should be washed in aged tank water only.

TANK

Before you change the water in your aquarium, you should clean the algae (if any) off the glass. There are numerous styles of algae scrapers available for this purpose, but a clean nylon scouring pad works just as well on glass aquaria.

A clean toothbrush, lashed to a cane, is very effective at cleaning awkward corners of the tank. Once you have scraped off the algae, it can be sucked from the gravel as part of a water change.

FILTER

Once a month, clean the filter, taking care to ensure you clean any impeller casing (which houses the little propeller that moves the water around), any pipes, and the intake grilles.

Algae will need to be scraped from the sides of the tank.

Clean any filter media by rinsing it thoroughly, using the water which you have just removed from the tank. Do not use fresh water, disinfectants or detergents, as these will destroy the vital filter bacteria. For the same reason, never clean the filter media too thoroughly.

If your filter media is very dirty, you may need to replace any disposable medium.

For this reason, it's a good idea to have the replacement media to hand. If a filter sponge becomes so clogged that it no longer works well, cut it in half and replace only half with a new sponge so that you retain some filter bacteria to speed up the maturation of the new media.

CLEANING THE DOUBLE INTERNAL FILTER

The double internal filter set-up requires a different cleaning and maintenance programme to the other types of filter. The presence of two filters allows you to clean one at a time, which helps to maintain a full working complement of bacteria in one filter.

Once every two weeks, clean the sponge inside one filter by rinsing it in the water which you removed as part of the water change.

Replace the filter. Two weeks later, do the same for the other filter, and repeat the process at two-weekly intervals.

SUBSTRATE

Goldfish keep their gravel substrate surprisingly clean, as they pick up the gravel grains in their mouths and suck them, removing any remains of food. However, despite this, the gravel will still need cleaning with every water change.

Overcleaning reduces the gravel's population of helpful filter bacteria. Undercleaning will result in blockages in the gravel and dead areas where no aerobic filter bacteria can grow.

The fishkeeper's two main tasks are to keep the aquarium clean and maintain water quality.

Overcleaning can be as dangerous to fish as undercleaning, so try to strike a healthy balance in your maintenance regime.

Cleaning should be carried out using a gravel vacuum – a siphon with a wide tube on the end. This cleans the gravel effectively, but does not suck it up the siphon tube – it falls back to the base of the tank. The siphoning activity removes the dirt, and then the gravel is re-deposited on the aquarium floor.

Planted substrates are best left alone, with perhaps just gentle siphoning of a thin layer of the surface to remove wastes and dead plant matter. The plants break down wastes very efficiently if undisturbed.

From time to time it may be necessary to rake the gravel over gently and to cover over any areas where the goldfish have dug too enthusiastically.

AIRPUMP

Every time you visit your tank, you should check the airpump by monitoring the bubbles produced from the airstone. There should be a constant and continuous flow of small bubbles.

Inside the airpump, a vibrating arm pulls a rubber diaphragm in and out to pump air into your tank. This rubber, exposed to heat and constantly moving, eventually wears out, so you should always keep a spare.

Occasionally airstones 'fur' up with calcium deposits or become otherwise blocked. If the air supply seems low, replace the airstone.

LIGHTS

Fluorescent lights tend to lose power after six to nine months, so should be replaced regularly. This is most important in planted tanks as the light is vital for their growth.

HEATER

If you use a heater set at its lowest level (as is likely in a goldfish tank), it will rarely be on and should last a very long time. Make sure it is attached in the correct, safe position and not knocked off its suckers on to the gravel.

The lights in a planted tank should be replaced regularly.

6

Pond Goldfish

There may come a time when you want to transfer your goldfish from the aquarium to the garden pond. This normally happens when the fish grow to be very large, but there is no reason why you cannot keep smaller common goldfish in a pond.

PLANNING YOUR POND

If you are going to keep your goldfish outside in a garden pond, you need to be sure that the pond in which they are going to live is suitable for them. There are a number of factors which affect suitability. These include:
• Location
• Size
• Depth
• Shape.

LOCATION

Your goldfish pond should be positioned so that it is not in direct sunlight, as this promotes the growth of algae. Suspended algae can colour the water so that you cannot see your fish. When it is filamentous algae (blanketweed) it can grow so thick that it clogs the pond and your equipment.

A patio pond with a wooden walkway.

SIZE

Goldfish should not be kept in very small ponds. Small bodies of water can quickly become polluted by wind-blown rubbish, and the water temperature can fluctuate dangerously.

Ideally, your goldfish pond should have a capacity of at least

450 UK gal/540.5 US fl gal
(2046 litres). This approximates to
a pond size of 6 feet x 6 feet (1.8
metres x 1.8 metres), and 2 feet
(60 cms) deep. Most gardens can
accommodate a pond of that size,
but, if yours cannot, reconsider
your decision to have a goldfish
pond.

DEPTH
Your pond should have a
minimum depth of 24 inches (60
cms). An adequate depth of water
helps to protect the goldfish from
extreme cold in the winter and
from surface predators.

SHAPE
Ponds can be any shape you like,
although it should be remembered
that very narrow ponds could have
poor water circulation. The best
pond designs include a deep area
where wastes collect, and the fish
can shelter, as well as a shallow
area for planting.

PREDATORS
In a garden setting, goldfish
predators include herons, snakes,
cats, foxes and mink. Swimming
dogs can also be a threat to your
fish, although this is because of
the likelihood of them puncturing
the liner, rather than any attempt

to catch and eat the fish.

Ponds also attract wildlife, and
some of these creatures may be
predators. There are reports of
grass snakes catching fish, and
even common garden birds
turning into 'kingfishers' to catch
fry – you may find a real
kingfisher coming to visit your
pond, too.

Unfortunately, there is little you
can do to protect your goldfish
from predators. Some fishkeepers
erect sheds or well-ventilated
greenhouses around their ponds,
but this is probably a little
extreme.

An alternative would be to
cover your pond with a net
(although unless the mesh is tiny,
this will prove no deterrent to
snakes). Some ponds are never
visited by predators.

BUILDING YOUR POND
Ponds break down into two types:
lined ponds and concrete ponds.
Both types are best built with an
external wall above ground level,
as raised sides prevent leaves and
rubbish from getting into the
pond, are some deterrent to
predators, make it more difficult
to accidentally fall into the pond,
and also provide somewhere to sit
and view your fish.

A pond designed with a waterfall, rocks and shrubbery.

LINED PONDS

As the name suggests, lined ponds consist of a sunken or raised hole, lined by a waterproof material. Liners may be flexible or rigid/pre-formed, and come in a variety of materials, although rubber, PVC, or, for rigid ponds, glass fibre, are the most common. Prices vary enormously, depending on liner thickness and the length of the guarantee.

FLEXIBLE LINERS

Flexible liners are thinner than the rigid pre-formed varieties, so an underlay is always laid first. This protects the liner from sharp stones or edges. The liner is put into place over the underlay, and the edges covered over with slabs or stones, or, in the case of a raised pond, the edges are brought up over blocks or bricks, and then covered.

The strength of the flexible liner is that it can be adapted to any shape or size you want. However, complicated pond designs will result in lots of creases and folds in the liner, which can trap dirt or even your fish, as well as making the pond more difficult to clean.

PRE-FORMED LINERS

Pre-formed pond liners are stronger, but more difficult to fit. The exact shape of the pond has to be marked out on the ground, and then excavated. The hole needs a layer of fine sand laid down before the pre-formed liner is fitted, and, once fitted, the liner has to be secured by backfilling the gap between the liner and the edges of the hole. Most pre-formed liners are in complex, curved shapes, rather than square, and few are an equal depth all over.

The benefit of pre-formed ponds is that they are very tough and durable. However, they are more expensive. It is also worth noting that the shapes are limited, many are not as deep as the recommended 2 feet (60 cms) and you may not be able to have a pond in the shape you want.

A raised octagon pond with wooden housing.

CONCRETE PONDS

Concrete ponds are the best choice for those wanting a larger pond. They are more expensive and more difficult to construct than lined ponds, ideally being built by a professional, but, when properly constructed, concrete ponds are strong and long-lasting.

Concrete ponds are normally built partly in and partly raised from the ground. They are usually made of bricks or blocks, lined with a layer of concrete. The concrete should be treated, to improve durability and water resistance, and then coated with water-resistant paint or a glass-fibre resin.

POND ACCESSORIES

Smaller ponds may not need any equipment, although a filter will improve water quality in ponds of all sizes.

Larger, or well-stocked ponds, may need a variety of equipment, such as a filter and a pump.

It is also a good idea to plant suitable vegetation in small ponds – lilies and other plants can do much of the job of breaking down wastes in small ponds.

FILTERS

Pond filters work in much the same way as aquarium filters (see page 24), but on a larger scale. The two main types of filter used in goldfish ponds are the standard black-box filter and the pressure filter.

BLACK-BOX FILTER

The black-box filter, the more popular of the two varieties, consists of a simple square container often with a fitted spraybar in the lid. The spraybar feeds water first through a sponge, and then through plastic filter media.

The filter is fed by a pump (see page 24), and water re-enters the pond by gravity. Consequently, this filter must be positioned above the water level of the pond, and water is pumped up to it.

The sponge component of the

A formal pond in a conservatory.

An informal pond with overhanging plants.

black-box filter should be regularly cleaned, by rinsing through with water from the pond. Some sophisticated black-box filters have separate compartments, perhaps containing brushes, which filter out larger waste before the water reaches the sponge.

PRESSURE FILTERS

Pressure filters have only become widely available comparatively recently. Unlike standard black-box filters, they can be positioned above or below the water's surface outside of the pond. Pressure filters are becoming increasingly popular because they can be buried or concealed out of sight.

PUMPS

If you have a filter, whether it returns water by gravity or under pressure, you will need a pump. The main requirement of a pump is that it is capable of pumping the full volume of water, through the filter, once in every hour. The pump should, ideally, be capable of pumping small, solid material with the water, so transporting wastes to the filter where they can be removed and/or broken down.

Make sure that your pump can reach sufficient 'head' (height) to reach the position of your filter. The head of your pump will be listed on the packaging – your filter cannot be higher than the head of the pump and still receive water. Remember, too, that most manufacturers list the optimum performance for a clean pump, so make allowances for any reduction in flow.

Pumps need an electrical supply, which may mean employing a professional electrician. Remember that some pumps use far more electricity than others, so always check the manufacturer's guidelines and ascertain what it will cost you to run the pump.

PLANTS
Any of the pond plants sold at your local aquatic shop will be suitable for a goldfish pond.

'Oxygenators' such as Hornwort *(Ceratophyllum demersum)*, Fishweed *(Lagarosiphon major)* or even the infamous clogger of waterways, Canadian Pondweed *(Elodea canadensis)*, are often recommended, but their oxygenating effect is overrated and they can quickly clog a small pond. All are best planted in removable baskets to keep them under control in the pond.

Water Lilies are ideal as they cover the surface, protecting the goldfish from predators and excluding some of the sunlight that can promote green water algae. Marginal plants like Water Primrose *(Caltha palustris)* also provide cover, and have bright yellow flowers in the early spring, and sometimes in the autumn, too.

Water Lilies make a beautiful addition to any garden pond, providing shade and protection for the fish.

Pond plants should be grown in a plant-growing medium held in baskets and topped off with heavy gravel. Even then some plants are very invasive and need trimming back and repotting regularly.

POND MANAGEMENT

Ponds do not require such intensive management as aquaria. However, it is important to control the growth of algae, and to ensure that the water quality is good.

ALGAE CONTROL

During spring and summer, algae builds up rapidly. Your fish can become obscured by pond water that has become thick and green. The one guaranteed way to

A pond does not require as much intensive management as an aquarium.

prevent this is to use an ultraviolet clarifier along with your filter.

The ultraviolet clarifier is positioned either between the pump and the filter, or in line from the outlet of the filter as it returns to the pond. Follow the manufacturer's suggestions.

Algae cells pass through the unit, their cell walls are disrupted and they are clumped together. As they pass through the filter, they are trapped by the sponge and broken down.

FEEDING

During the spring and summer months, it is not always necessary to feed your fish if they live in a well-cultivated and well-managed pond. Most pond owners, however, do feed, as it is a chance to interact with your goldfish and to check them. Very heavily stocked ponds will also benefit from feeding through the summer months. Your goldfish will be hungrier at summer temperatures and will digest food more easily and faster.

A flourishing, well-planted pond will attract large amounts of terrestrial and aquatic insects, which may provide the main part of your goldfishes' diet. Pond-dwelling goldfish will feed on live

Diet can be supplemented with floating pond pellets.

creatures from the bottom of the pond and on the plants.

Your goldfish will also eat daphnia in mid-water, and come to the surface to eat hatching midge pupae, or terrestrial insects that have fallen on the water.

Between May and September, when the water warms, you can feed your goldfish with flake or floating pond pellets. In a heavily stocked goldfish pond, extra feeding ensures good growth and colour and increases the chance of your fish breeding.

During colder periods, your goldfish may go into semi-hibernation, settling themselves in

any silt on the bottom of the pond, and remaining there until the weather becomes warmer. They may wake up for short periods in warmer weather, but feeding them is usually unnecessary and may even be harmful as goldfish are not able to digest food easily at lower temperatures.

SPAWNING

In a pond holding more than two or three fish, it is almost inevitable that spawning will take place. This usually happens between April and July.

Spawning usually occurs early in

the morning, or late in the evening. If you watch your fish during the spawning period, you will see the males chasing the females. Eventually, the females will be driven into the cover of plants and blanketweed, where they will lay their eggs. The males will then fertilise the eggs.

In warm weather, the eggs develop within four to five days, although some will be eaten before this time, even by their parents. The newly hatched fry will be swimming independently within 48 hours, gaining their nutrition from tiny food items in the pond.

The goldfish fry will be the same dark-brown colour as their ancestors, and will only develop the typical orange colour after one to two years.

Pond-dwelling goldfish grow relatively slowly in comparison to aquarium-kept fry. This is due to

Males (left) will chase females during the spawning period.

lower temperatures in the pond, and natural food which is less high in protein.

However, the difference in diet and temperature, and a life spent swimming in green algal soup is often responsible for producing fish with more vivid coloration than their aquarium counterparts.

'FOSTERING' FISH FRY

In a pond environment, a large proportion of the fish fry will die. Some will be eaten, some will develop fatal illnesses, and others will die as a result of some deformity.

This is all part of natural selection, but you can increase the number of fry that survive by collecting some of the spawned eggs and hatching them in an aquarium. You should keep the eggs in an outbuilding, where temperatures stay relatively cool, as this will help them to better

Spawning usually takes place in the early morning or late evening.

make the transition back to the pond.

The aquarium-kept fry will need small amounts of specialist foods like baby brineshrimp and commercial egg-layer fry foods. Once the fry's mouths are large enough, you can feed them on fine powdered flake, then standard flake and all the foods recommended for adults. The fry will be ready to go back to the pond once they are 2 inches (5 cms) long.

7 *Goldfish Behaviour*

U nless you meet a talking fish, understanding everything that fish do is impossible. Applying human intentions and emotions to your fish can be misleading. So, how can you gain a better understanding of your fish's behaviour?

WHY DOES HE...
Here are some goldfish behavioural patterns you may see, and some possible explanations for them.

STAND ON HIS NOSE?
In the wild, Crucians or Gibel

Black and Gold Telescope Eye: a fancy two-tailed variety.

Ryukin: an elegant, graceful mover.

carp move carefully over the lake bed searching for tidbits. As they investigate each area they tip up, so that their tail is held high.

Other members of the shoal interpret this position as indicating the presence of nearby food. They respond by swimming over to join the feast, and also hold their tails high as they feed – a signal to any other members of the shoal. Today's goldfish still perform such actions instinctively.

CHASE OTHER FISH?

Sometimes, you may observe male goldfish chasing other goldfish, male and female alike. This normally happens immediately prior to spawning, when gravid females exude hormonal signals. The males react by pursuing the female, trying to be the first to fertilise her eggs.

In the absence of pregnant females, the same response can be elicited by fish with a 'pregnant' body shape. This is why commons and fancies may not be an ideal mix in your aquarium. Many of the fancy goldfish varieties have a rounded body shape, and at

A common goldfish (lemon): a single-tailed variety.

certain times of the year, or when the right combination of light, temperature and water changes triggers them off, male commons can spend all their time chasing these seemingly pregnant fish – putting the fancies under a significant degree of stress.

GREET ME?
When you approach your tank, your goldfish may rise to the surface. Many fishkeepers believe that their fish recognise them, and that rising to the surface is the fish's way of saying hello.

It is unlikely that your goldfish recognise your face. Instead, it is the movement of your body towards the tank (and the food pot) which is familiar to them.

They associate your arrival with food, and rise to the surface in hungry anticipation. It is a simple learned response. Nevertheless, it is fun to see your goldfish react in this way, and, if nothing else, it proves that your goldfish are hungry and healthy.

RACE AROUND THE TANK?
Racing around the tank is not normal – unstressed Goldfish normally move with steady grace. A fish moving erratically may be experiencing fits. The cause may be a vitamin deficiency, a major health problem in the fish's nervous system, or electrical discharges from your aquarium equipment could be to blame.

A few fish have regular episodes

of fitting, which do not appear to harm them, and they lead otherwise normal lives between these episodes.

CHANGE COLOUR?

Young goldfish are a bronze colour. As they age, they develop the more vibrant reds, oranges and golds traditionally associated with goldfish. White-coloured fish with patches of colour may turn completely white, while a few have turned bright orange.

In fact, excepting albino fish, which have no pigmentation, all goldfish will change colour throughout their lives, some more noticeably than others. Many goldfish lose colour as they age.

A Calico Fantail: one of the most natural and healthy of the twin-tailed varieties.

8 Health Care

Goldfish are hardier than many of the tropical fish species. A sick goldfish will usually survive long enough for you to treat it, unlike the smaller tropicals which often die with no apparent warning. Observing your goldfish on a twice-daily basis should alert you to any developing problems and give you time to overcome them.

Many goldfish health problems can be cured with the right remedy from your aquatic shop. Vets who understand fish problems are not as common as most fishkeepers would like, but, if you find one, make use of him or her for problems that defy diagnosis or that may require antibiotics.

WARNING SIGNS

If your fish display any of the following symptoms, you need to take prompt action.

Close observation of your goldfish will mean that you spot problems at an early stage.

Overcrowding causes stress to fish and may well upset the water balance.

- Clamped fins, i.e. fins which are held down and close to the body.
- Swimming on the spot, known as 'shimmying' when performed by tropical fish.
- Gasping or biting at the surface.
- Listless behaviour or lying stationary in the water.
- Scales slightly raised from the body.
- Reddened or sore spots on the fish's body.
- White, red, or black marks, other than those due to normal pigmentation, on the body or fins and tail.
- Any marks on the mouth or lips.
- Wrongly aligned jaws.
- Eyes which appear cloudy or dull.
- Loss of appetite.

POLLUTION

Major causes of fish ill-health include overfeeding, overstocking, inadequate or faulty equipment, poor tapwater, and insufficient water changes.

If your fish display any of the above symptoms, your first step should be to test water quality. Test for ammonia and nitrites first, followed by pH and nitrate tests if the first tests do not reveal anything. If a fish looks healthy, but is behaving oddly, and the above tests are all clear, try 24 hours of extra aeration and carbon-filter the aquarium in case chemicals contained in your tapwater are behind the problem.

Only after ruling out poor-quality water, should you contemplate adding medicinal chemicals to the water.

A goldfish
suffering from
tail rot.

SKIN COMPLAINTS

Most skin complaints are easily
treated. Some of the more
common ones are dealt with here.

CARP POX

Carp pox usually occurs in early
spring. It is a non-infectious viral
condition, seemingly triggered by
temperature fluctuations. This may
explain why it is far more
common in ponds than aquaria.

Symptoms of the condition
include white waxy nodules,
which can appear anywhere on the
fish's body.

This complaint is rarely
dangerous, and usually disappears
of its own accord, although it has
been known to recur.

Fish that suffer from recurrent
bouts normally grow out of the
disease as they age.

FIN/TAIL ROT AND MOUTH 'FUNGUS'

Both of these complaints are
caused by bacterial infections,
usually occurring as a result of
poor-quality water. The first
symptoms appear as white marks
on the edges of the fins and the
mouth. This is quickly followed
by a reddening of the area, which
precedes the rotting away of the
affected parts.

Fungal infections are relatively easy to
cure. Pictured: fungus on the
damaged eye of a goldfish.

While it is possible to cure the problem, prevention is by far the better option. Think carefully about how you can improve water quality and the cleanliness of your substrate – dirty gravel has been implicated in these problems.

CUTS AND GRAZES

Equipment or tank decor with sharp edges may damage your fish as they swim past. Most incidents occur when fish are chasing or being chased at speed. Dead skin and disturbed scales, produced as the result of a graze, may turn white. If this happens, you should treat the water with a general antibacterial agent, to prevent the wound from becoming infected. If left untreated, infected cuts and grazes could develop into a fungal infection or become ulcerated and may require antibiotic treatments from a vet.

FUNGAL INFECTIONS

Fungus often develops on a wound, feeding on the damaged skin or scales. Fungal infections appear markedly different from other white-coloured skin complaints, looking much like strands or clumps of cotton wool (cotton). Fungal infections are relatively easy to cure, but

remember that the wound underneath may need attention.

SORES AND ULCERS

Sores or ulcers may be caused by a bacterial or viral infection. An ulcer can develop on the site of an infected wound, but other ulcers seem to break out from internal infections. One school of thought suggests the involvement of a virus in these outbreaks, which weakens the fish's immune system.

Many ulcers stemming from wounds can be successfully treated with an external antibacterial agent. However, some 'internal' ulcer problems recur over several years, eventually with fatal results.

It may be possible to eradicate the problem completely with an antibiotic treatment, either in food or as an additive in the water. Your vet will advise you about appropriate forms of treatment.

Some ulcers can be treated with an antibacterial agent.

Twin-tailed goldfish variety: Fantail (nymph).

Viruses are untreatable, but the bacteria may be held at bay.

EXCESSIVE SCRATCHING/TWITCHING

Occasional scratching or twitching is normal in a healthy fish, but excessive amounts of either indicate a problem. Fish may flick and scratch themselves against the aquarium decor and equipment in a bid to relieve the irritation.

If there is a visible sign of the irritation, such as reddened skin, an antibacterial treatment may prevent the inflamed skin developing sores or ulcers.

Fish will also flick and scratch and may develop a heavy coat of mucus when ammonia or nitrite are high. Make an immediate water change and find out what is wrong with your filter. Have you been overfeeding?

White spots or white patches of slime may harbour parasites. Whitespot – tiny pin-head blobs of white on the fins and body, each harbouring a parasite – is easy to treat. Most of the other parasites can clearly be seen with the naked eye or a hand glass, and are treatable (see page 74).

Do not use a cocktail of treatments, unless your vet has instructed you to. Multi-treatments can cause unpleasant side effects. Some remedies may reduce the oxygen content of the water, so extra aeration is a good idea.

It has been suggested that excessive twitching and other odd behaviour may be caused by electricity, discharged from old or poorly maintained equipment. This type of problem has been reported from time to time, the main culprits being lighting systems and internal filters and heaters. Check the cables with great care, especially where they enter the equipment.

SPAWNING TUBERCULES

During the spawning period, male goldfish develop 'coursing stars' or tubercules. These are white marks on the gill plates, which are harmless. They should not be confused with other, more serious health problems.

WEN SLIME

Fancy goldfish varieties, such as the Oranda or Lionhead, often develop white-coloured excretions in the 'folds' of the hood. These excretions are usually harmless, but should be checked to make sure they are not anything more serious, such as fungus growing on a wound.

PARASITIC INFECTIONS

There are numerous parasites which affect goldfish, of which Whitespot is the most common. If your goldfish have spent any time in an outdoor pool, they may also be affected by parasites such as leeches, fish lice and anchor worms.

An adult Calico Fantail, showing the characteristic fan-shaped tail.

WHITESPOT

Whitespot is caused by *Ichthyopthirius multifiliis,* a parasite that burrows underneath the goldfish's skin, forming the white pin-head cysts that give this illness its name. Other symptoms of the disease include gill irritation and consequent gasping at the water surface.

Whitespot is usually easy to cure with a chemical treatment. When the cysts burst, the Whitespot parasite begins the free-swimming stage of its life cycle, and it is during this stage that the chemical additive takes effect.

Keeping your fish warm, although not so warm as to decrease the oxygen content of the water, will speed up the life cycle of the parasite, so that eradication can take place in a shorter time period.

Always treat the whole aquarium or pond, rather than individual fish.

LEECHES

Leeches are easy to recognise, being slim, worm-like creatures with segmented, sometimes stripy, bodies. Leeches fix themselves to the skin and suck nourishment from the fish. They lay tough little egg packages in the aquarium or pond.

In a pond environment, leeches can be almost impossible to eradicate. A specialised treatment, available from your aquatic store, will keep the leeches under control, but it is unlikely to solve the problem completely as the egg pouches protect the next generation of leeches until the medication breaks down.

Affected aquarium fish are much easier to treat. Such fish should be bathed in a salt-water solution. You can either use a proprietary solution, following the manufacturer's instructions, or, you can create your own.

A solution of 1 oz (30 g) of cooking (not table) or marine salt, dissolved in 1.75 pint (1 litre) of water, works just as well.

The fish should bathe in the solution for 10 minutes, following which the leeches should drop off or be easily removed using tweezers.

The salt-water solution has the added benefit of treating the small wounds which the leeches leave behind – as a precaution you could also use a general antibacterial agent as the wounds heal.

FISH LOUSE

The fish louse, or *Argulus,* attaches itself to your goldfish's body and sucks juices from it. Unlike the leech, the fish louse is hard to spot, being flat and scale-like in appearance. Often, a louse infestation is only noticed once the fish is covered with them. A broad-spectrum anti-parasite remedy will remove lice quickly and effectively.

ANCHOR WORMS

Anchor worms have short, slim, pale-brown bodies, which look similar to leeches. They are easily destroyed by a general anti-parasite treatment.

Alternatively, the individual worms can be pulled off using tweezers, and an antibacterial agent then added to the water to prevent infection of the wounds left by the worms.

OTHER ILLNESSES

Although skin complaints and parasite infestations account for the majority of fish health problems, there are a number of other problems which you should be aware of. These are outlined overleaf.

Bubble Eye: a fancy twin-tailed variety for the specialist fishkeeper.

DROPSY

Dropsy is very distressing. It causes the fish to swell up, making the scales lift, which gives the fish the appearance of an open pine cone. The condition may also cause the eyes to swell.

Dropsy has a number of causes, a common one being old age. The organs of elderly fish tend to be less efficient, which can result in an imbalance of the osmotic system – liquid can flow into the fish, but not out again. Bacterial and viral infections, which damage vital organs, are other common causes, although the condition can also be brought about by nutritional deficiencies.

Dropsy is extremely difficult to treat, and many fish do not survive – the damage inflicted on the internal organs is often too severe for a full recovery to be made. If the disease is caught early, and the fish is young and otherwise healthy, antibiotics may be effective.

POPPING EYES

Some fancies have telescopic or protruding eyes, but if a goldfish's eye swells for no apparent reason, it usually indicates an illness, such as dropsy, an infection, or physical damage to the fish's head.

Like dropsy, the problem is usually internal, which can make it difficult to treat. The best general treatment is an antibacterial agent, but this is another area where a trip to the vet and antibiotics may be helpful.

In some cases, the eye may be permanently damaged, or may even fall out. If this happens, it may not affect the fish's general level of health and quality of life, but take care to ensure that the fish is not missing out at feeding time.

TUMOURS

Goldfish get benign and malignant growths inside and outside of the body. The best and only treatment is to watch and wait, although the fish should be kept in a quarantine tank in case the lump is due to infection.

BUOYANCY PROBLEMS

Fancy goldfish, with their strangely-shaped bodies, seem especially prone to buoyancy problems. It appears that the body shape causes pressure to build up on the fish's swimbladder – a gas-filled internal organ that governs the height at which the fish swims in the water.

A Wakin: a twin-tailed variety with an elongated body, from whom the Veil Tail is derived.

Filled with gas, the swimbladder will force the fish to the surface of the water. When empty, the fish will be able to swim just above the substrate.

Another explanation is that trapped gas (i.e. indigestion) is the cause of the problem (again the body shape may play a part). A steady diet of flake or pellet food only seems to increase the likelihood of the problem occurring.

A possible cure is increasing the amount of roughage in the diet. Blanched vegetables and (especially) chopped earthworms seem to help. Feeding more natural foods all the time can help to prevent the problem.

Other treatments worth trying are raising the tank temperature a little, or moving the fish to a warmer tank, at, for example, 70 degrees Fahrenheit (21.5 degrees Celsius), adding salt to the water at one teaspoon per UK/US gallon (or one teaspoon per quater litre), and, if all else fails, using antibacterial treatments.

Even if the problem cannot be overcome, swimbladder problems may not overly affect your fish. Provided that the fish concerned receives its fair share of food, and is not harassed by the other fish, it will carry on quite happily. Euthanasia is not necessary.

London Shubunkin, similar in all but colour to the common goldfish.

OXYGEN DEFICIENCY

Lack of oxygen in the water may be caused by inadequate filtration or water movement. Another cause is too high a water temperature, as warm water holds far less oxygen than cold.

If there is insufficient oxygen in your aquarium, your fish may hover next to airstones and filter outlets, or gasp or bite at the water surface, referred to as *hana-age* by Japanese fishkeepers. This is an attempt to increase their oxygen intake.

If your fish display any of these symptoms, run an emergency aeration of the aquarium, while you try to diagnose the specific cause. Poor-quality aquarium water could also be behind the problem, so perform all those water tests again!

GRAVEL IN THE MOUTH

Not strictly an illness, but a very common problem. Goldfish will mouth over the gravel, and, if the gravel is the wrong shape or size, the fish may get pieces stuck in their mouths. A crooked mouth, or an inability to feed despite obvious interest, may be clues.

Generally, gravel can be removed with care by the goldfish owner. Wrap the fish in a wet cloth, covering its eyes, and use fine tweezers to remove the gravel. If you are nervous about this, any vet, not just a fish specialist, will be used to dealing with the problem.

TREATMENTS

There is a vast range of treatments available, mostly in liquid form, designed to be added to the aquarium or pond. You should take care to aerate the tank sufficiently while fish are under treatment.

Once the fish has recovered, medication can be removed by carbon filtration, followed by a large water change. Test the water regularly for ammonia and nitrite as your filter bacteria may be damaged by some treatments occasionally.

DEATHS

Unfortunately, not every disease will be treatable, and not every fish will survive. When you are faced with a dead fish, you must remove it from the water

Fantails: a hardy fancy fish.

immediately. Decomposing fish will result in pollution.

Sometimes, you may be faced with a dead fish in your tank, despite the fact that there is no infection or problem that you are aware of. All fishkeepers face this problem at some point, no matter how experienced they are and however good their filtration and water quality.

Usually, the fish concerned has died from natural causes, such as old age, a heart attack or a stroke. In such cases, remove the fish from the tank, check for signs of illness, and test the water for raised ammonia or nitrite levels.

EUTHANASIA

It is extremely difficult to judge when a goldfish has had enough and is genuinely unlikely to recover from a disease.

Ulcers can leave a fish totally debilitated with little hope of recovery. Large internal or external growths can have the same effect. Some mouth problems can leave a fish unable to feed properly. Multiple disease problems, such as slimy skin, ulcers, and fungus combined, may point to major problems internally.

If you decide that your fish is beyond help, the kindest method of euthanasia is a simple blow to the head. Lots of other methods are suggested, but many are more concerned with the fish owner's feelings than the fish, and some, like freezing the fish to death, are downright cruel.

A HAPPY ENDING

Goldfish are tough and beautiful. You may never experience health problems with them if you look after them properly. So enjoy them – healthy fish can live for 20 years and become a constant and enduring pleasure.